Make an Egg Card

Catherine Baker

Contents

You Can Make an Egg Card

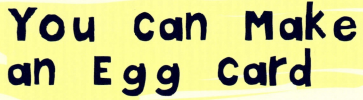

You need these things!

2

Make the Card

1 Cut out a big circle.

2 Cut out a little circle.

3 Add these bits to make a chick.

4 Cut out a big egg.

5 Cut a zig-zag in the egg.

zig-zag

6 Draw on the top of the egg.

7 Put a pin in the egg.

pin

8 Put tape under the chick.

tape

9 Stick the chick in the egg.

Put your friend's name
on the card.

To Jess

The Egg Card

An egg card for your friend!

To Jess